I0155620

Caring for Aging Parents

From Struggle to Strength

Quick Tips to Avoid Mental Burnout, Financial Bailout, and Family Fallouts

By Monica J. Gilliam, M.Ed.

Copyright © 2024 Monica J. Gilliam, M.Ed.

All rights reserved. No part of this publication may be reproduced, distributed, or transmitted in any form or by any means, including photocopying, recording, or other electronic or mechanical methods, without the prior written permission of the publisher, except in the case of brief quotations embodied in critical reviews and certain other noncommercial uses permitted by copyright law.

This book is dedicated to my parents, Louis and Eruline. Thank you for allowing me to grow in my role as a caregiver and evolve from struggle to strength.

To Sophia P. and Andrea O., I'm thankful we've built a caregiver sisterhood that is strong on faith and friendship. Thank you to The Peeples Family for always supporting me, mom, and dad. Sara N. thank you for the confirmation. Finally, to Mother Mat, thank you for praying with and for me.

"To God be the glory for the things He has done."

Table of Contents

Chapter 1: Understanding the Role of a Caregiver

✳

As you start the journey of caregiving for your aging parents, it's vital to have a good understanding of the role you're undertaking. Whether you volunteered or stumbled into this position, relevant information will help you navigate this season of your life. In this first chapter, we'll explore what it truly means to be a caregiver, the emotional and physical toll it can take, and how societal and cultural factors shape the caregiving experience.

What It Means to Be a Caregiver for an Aging Parent

Caring for your parents involves providing physical, emotional, and often financial support to someone who needs assistance due to illness, disability, or old age. When it comes to caring for an aging parent, the responsibilities can vary widely, ranging from helping with tasks like bathing, dressing, grocery shopping, and cooking to managing medication, and paying bills.

At its core, caregiving is an act of love and compassion. It also comes with its share of challenges and sacrifices. Being a caregiver requires patience, empathy, and a willingness to adapt to the changing needs of your parents as they get older.

Acknowledging the Societal and Cultural Aspects of Caregiving

The role of a caregiver is not solely determined by individual circumstances; it's also influenced by broader societal and cultural factors. In many cultures, caregiving for aging parents is considered a duty for the family and a sign of respect for elders. However, cultural expectations can place undue pressure on adult children, leading to feelings of obligation and even guilt if they're unable to meet perceived expectations.

Societal attitudes toward aging and caregiving can impact the resources available to care providers. For example, affluent communities have plenty of support systems in place to meet the needs of their elderly, while less affluent communities lack resources and support services, often leaving caregivers feeling isolated and overwhelmed. For example, let's look at medical transportation services. Free transportation (offered by nonprofit organizations or community agencies) to medical appointments may be available in upper-and middle-class neighborhoods, but in communities of great health disparities, this service may not be available.

No matter which end of the economic spectrum your family is on, remember, you're not alone on this journey. According to the Center for Disease Control in 2020 there were approximately 53 million caregivers in the United States. By gaining a deeper understanding of the caregiver role, you can better prepare yourself for the road ahead.

Recognizing the Emotional and Physical Toll of Caregiving

Caregiving is not just about attending to the physical needs of your aging parent; it also involves navigating a range of complex emotions and experiences. Many caregivers experience feelings of stress, anxiety, guilt, and grief as they witness the decline of their parent's health. The struggle to meet the caregiver's own needs while balancing other responsibilities can be equally challenging.

Moreover, the physical demands of taking care of your parents can take a toll on your own well-being. Sleep deprivation, lack of exercise, eating poorly, and neglecting your own medical needs are common pitfalls for caregivers, leading to increased risk of chronic illness, burnout, and depression.

To combat provider burnout let's identify five activities you will do this month for your physical and mental well-being. A few examples include taking a fifteen to twenty-minute walk at least twice a week, going to a gym, spending a night in a hotel (stay-cation), signing up for a monthly massage package, or trying yoga for stress management. Use the space below to plan your first five self-care activities. List the date, activity, and check the completed box when you successfully complete the task. This chart will help you make taking care of yourself a priority. As a care provider it is easy to forget about your own wellbeing.

Date	Activity	Completed

"True caregiving is giving your all to someone who can't reciprocate and that doesn't influence the love you continue to give." *Monica J. Gilliam*

Chapter 2: Financial Challenges Faced by Caregivers

※

One of the most significant challenges for caregivers is managing the financial costs associated with being the primary provider. Medical related expenses like doctor visit co-pays, parking fees, prescription refills, and home modifications can quickly add up causing financial burdens. Many caregivers find themselves dipping into their savings, reducing their work hours, or even quitting their jobs altogether to accommodate caring for their parents.

My experience as a full-time caregiver of two parents was a major financial strain. I tried keeping a traditional job with regular hours. Over the years I took time off from work three different times under Family Medical Leave Act (FMLA). However, this past year I still needed more time off because of the frequency of my parents' medical appointments, emergency room visits, and hospital stays. That is when I came to the realization that I had to resign from my full-time job to effectively care for my parents.

FMLA may secure your job, but once you use all your paid time off (PTO), any additional time off will be deducted from your check. There have been times when I used all my PTO and my check was only a couple of hundred dollars for a two-week pay period. Financial hardships are significant. Consequently, it is important to have a financial plan before transitioning from gainful employment into the role of full-time or part-time caregiver.

Tips for Managing Finances:

- If you anticipate having to resign or reduce your work hours, start paying off or paying down your debt.

- Consider paying bills a few months in advance.

- If you must resign from your full-time job, you don't want to exhaust all your savings to supplement your reduced or non-existent caregiver income. Consider an additional source of income, such as part-time work or freelance opportunities. Get your side hustles on…and quick!

- Communicate honestly with family members about needing financial support to maintain your household while you are in the primary caregiver role. Be prepared to disclose your bank statements and other expenses.

- If your parents have disposable income and you have resigned or greatly reduced your work hours to care for them, ask if they are willing to help supplement your income with a weekly or monthly stipend.

*Date:*_____

*Time:*_____

Chapter Reflections

1. One thought from this chapter that resonates with me is:

_____
_____
_____
_____
_____
_____

2. One concept from this chapter that I will implement within a week is:

_____
_____
_____
_____
_____
_____

3. One positive thought, affirmation, or kind word I want to say to myself today is:

_____
_____
_____
_____
_____
_____

Chapter 3: Balancing Work, Family, and Caregiving

Balancing the demands of work, family, and caring for your parents can feel like a juggling act for many care providers. The pressure to maintain all areas of your personal life can lead to feelings of inadequacy.

Studies have shown that taking time for yourself is the key to being a loving, patient care provider. I often use a cell phone analogy when talking to caregivers about self-care. When your cell phone battery is getting low the quality of the call is compromised. Many times, the reception is bad, and you have to start yelling "can you hear me?" Recharging the phone is the only solution for it to resume functioning at an optimal level. As the caregiver for your parents, you too have likely felt rundown and experienced guilt about the times when you didn't feel successful in your caregiver role. You may feel impatient. While you may not yell, it's possible you are raising your voice or using a condescending tone. If you find yourself feeling this way, just like the cell phone, you need to recharge. Here are a few ideas to help you recenter your physical, mental, and spiritual health for a more balanced work and family life balance.

Tips for Achieving Balance:

- Do what you can in one day and finish the rest of the task on another day. You may not be able to complete everything the way you "normally" would. Accept that you are experiencing a "new normal."

- Communicate with your employer about your caregiving responsibilities and explore flexible work arrangements. Inquire about working remotely. I found going into the office provided the socialization and respite I needed from being at my parent's home 24/7. There is no right or wrong way to manage traditional work responsibilities. Do what works best for you.

- Listen to spiritual music, sermons, or podcasts to connect to a higher power to give you strength and guidance.

- Read your Bible or other spiritual text.

- Set boundaries and learn to say no to non-essential requests. I remember a celebrity saying "no" is a complete sentence. Practice saying the word "No." No to family members and to your parents. They too can be demanding of your time.

Here are examples of how to practice saying "No."

Responses to Family Members

- *"No, I can't sit with mom today. We made the schedule weeks ago and I have plans for today. I can switch days next week, but not today."*

- *"No, I can't cook your favorite dish for Thanksgiving dinner. I have to sit with Dad. I'm happy to pick up a dessert or two from the local bakery. What desserts would you like me to buy?"*

Responses to Your Parents

- *"No, I am not going to the store today. I see you have groceries here. I will go to the store on XYZ day. Let's make a list of items you want from the store so I can get them the next time I go grocery shopping."*

- *"No, I can't do that task now, because I'm tired. I'll be happy to do it for you after I have gotten some rest. I'm going to take a nap for a few hours. I'll call you when I wake up. Call me if there is an emergency."*

"Continue to talk about your caregiver journey—even if your truth makes others uncomfortable."   Monica J. Gilliam

Date:_____

Time:_____

Chapter Reflections

1. One thought from this chapter that resonates with me is:

_____

_____

_____

_____

_____

_____

2. One concept from this chapter that I will implement within a week is:

_____

_____

_____

_____

_____

_____

3. One positive thought, affirmation, or kind word I want to say to myself today is:

_____

_____

_____

_____

_____

_____

Chapter 4: Managing Your Emotions

Caregiving can evoke a wide range of emotions, including guilt over not being able to do all the things you want to do to make your parents comfortable. You may also experience fear and uncertainty over a recent diagnosis your parent received. These feelings are entirely normal.

As a caregiver, you will experience highs and lows. The highs certainly help sustain you through the lows. Having patience and empathy for your aging parent is necessary when dealing with emotionally fragile seniors. Sometimes they may cry for no apparent reason, but the truth is they miss their family and friends. Many have outlived their parents, siblings, and childhood friends. They yearn for their independence. Parents remember the days when they could drive themselves to the store and run weekend errands. The loss of autonomy may trigger negative behavior toward the caregiver. Do not take it personally. People often take out their frustration on those closest to them. The old saying "hurt people hurt people" comes to mind.

Tips for Handling Emotions:

- Practice self-compassion. Remind yourself you are doing the best you can and that is enough.

- It is okay to cry, cry, and cry some more. Being a caregiver is hard. Often you wake up one day to find out you are the designated caregiver of mom and dad. There was no conversation or vote, you just ended up caring for your parents and now it's your full-time responsibility.

- Seek support from a therapist or life coach who can provide a listening ear and offer a new perspective regarding your caregiver experiences. It is beneficial having a professional to assist you in managing your thoughts and feelings.

- Prioritize self-care activities (add an activity to your calendar this week from your list of five options in chapter one) to recharge your physical, mental, and emotional health.

- Join a support group for caregivers where you can connect with others who recognize what you're going through.

- Address challenges and concerns when they arise or within a week. Unresolved issues can be a breeding ground for negative behavior and emotions.

*Date:*_____

*Time:*_____

Chapter Reflections

1. One thought from this chapter that resonates with me is:

_____

_____

_____

_____

_____

_____

2. One concept from this chapter that I will implement within a week is:

_____

_____

_____

_____

_____

_____

3. One positive thought, affirmation, or kind word I want to say to myself today is:

_____

_____

_____

_____

_____

_____

Chapter 5: Navigating Family Dynamics and Conflicts

※

Family dynamics play a significant role in caregiving. Relatives may not fully understand the extent of your responsibilities as the primary caregiver. Some relatives might criticize your decision regarding your parents, yet they do not offer to help or find any resolution to what they deem to be the problem.

Communicating with family about shared responsibilities requires skills and patience. Some would rather walk over hot coals than have this discussion with siblings, aunts, or uncles. The truth is, there is no easy way to have this conversation. A family meeting is inevitable. Before having a family meeting about shared duties it's important to have realistic expectations. Be mindful that you may not leave the meeting with the support you want. Be open to compromise and don't discount small victories.

Tips for Navigating Family Conflicts:

- Initiate open and honest communication with family members about your parents' needs and your caregiving role.

- Schedule the family meeting in person or via an online platform like Zoom, TEAMS, or even FaceTime.

- Make the meeting short and distribute an agenda at the beginning of the meeting so the conversation does not go off the rails. Every family has one relative who wants to take over the meeting with negative remarks. Redirect the comments. Keep the tone of the meeting positive and end with a solution or at least initial steps to improve the situation.

- Clarify expectations and responsibilities to ensure everyone understands the family plan moving forward.

- When possible, seek an ally before the meeting so you are not the only person advocating that the caregiver duties be shared by other relatives.

- Focus on finding answers and working together as a team to provide the best possible care for your aging family member.

- Address unresolved issues with your parents. It is difficult to care for a parent when harboring ill feelings. It is also difficult for a parent to cooperate with the adult child/caregiver if they too are dealing with complex emotions.

Here is a list of caregiver duties you can ask other family members to assist you with:

1. Managing medication refills, picking up prescriptions, or scheduling home deliveries

2. Grocery shopping

3. Taking parents to the barber/beauty salon or nail shop

4. Scheduling and taking parents to medical appointments

5. Cooking or meal preparation

6. Washing and folding loads of laundry

7. Taking parents to worship service

8. Coordinating home maintenance including AC checks and lawn care

9. Getting the vehicles inspected

10. Taking parents out to socialize (movies, ice cream, lunch, walks)

"I know you don't recognize the person in the mirror. What happened to your hair, clothes, weight…and joy? Ask for help. As much as you would like, you can't do this alone."

Monica J. Gilliam

---

*Date:*_____

*Time:*_____

Chapter Reflections

1. One thought from this chapter that resonates with me is:

_____
_____
_____
_____
_____
_____

2. One concept from this chapter that I will implement within a week is:

_____
_____
_____
_____
_____
_____

3. One positive thought, affirmation, or kind word I want to say to myself today is:

_____
_____
_____
_____
_____
_____

Chapter 6: Identifying Sources of Support

✳

Caregiving can feel like a solitary journey, but it doesn't have to be. Building a strong support system is essential to help navigate the road ahead.

Support can come from neighbors, support groups, and healthcare professionals. Identifying and tapping into these resources can provide invaluable emotional, practical, and even financial assistance to help lighten the load.

Neighbors:

- Neighbors are an excellent resource for support because your parents are already familiar with them. There is a preexisting trust factor.

- Reach out to neighbors who may be willing to lend a helping hand by sitting with your parents or running errands for them.

- Neighbors can conduct wellness checks on your parents if they do not answer the phone when you call.

- Be specific with neighbors about the type of assistance you need, whether it's helping with household chores, running errands, or rolling out the trash and recycling containers on trash pick-up day.

Support Groups:

- Joining a support group for caregivers can provide a sense of camaraderie and understanding from others who are going through similar experiences.

- Look for local or online support groups that focus specifically on caregivers of aging parents, where you can share experiences, exchange tips, and offer support to one another.

- Ask your church leaders to start a ministry to support and pray for caregivers. There is a great opportunity for the ministry to expand and help support adult children who are caring for their parents.

- Starting October 2024, you can join my virtual parent caregiver support group on the first Thursday of each month; from 7 p.m. to 7:45 p.m. CST. Send an email to admin@thecaregiver-consultant.com for the Zoom link. Be sure to put "Caregiver Meeting" in the subject line. Space is limited.

Healthcare Professionals:

- Contact healthcare professionals, such as your parent's doctor, physician's assistant, or social worker about geriatric health concerns. They are a great resource for information.

- Medical professionals provide important information about your parents' condition. They can connect you with community resources, medical specialists, and offer expertise on managing your caregiving responsibilities.

*Date:*_____

*Time:*_____

Chapter Reflections

1. One thought from this chapter that resonates with me is:

_____

_____

_____

_____

_____

2. One concept from this chapter that I will implement within a week is:

_____

_____

_____

_____

_____

3. One positive thought, affirmation, or kind word I want to say to myself today is:

_____

_____

_____

_____

_____

Chapter 7: Effectively Communicating Your Needs

Effective communication is necessary to build a support system that meets your needs as a provider. Clearly articulating your concerns and preferences can help others understand how they can best support you in this role. When individuals offer to help, immediately have them commit to a date, time, and activity. It is easy to let a casual conversation be just that. A word of caution. Do not end the communication there. Now is not the time to be bashful or prideful. Ask for and accept help!

We've all heard the expression "the squeaky wheel gets the oil." To loosely translate this saying, it means if you don't express your need, the need will not be met. Many people have been raised to "grin and bear it" or told "don't complain" or "don't beg anyone to help you." There is a difference between begging and asking. Here is my question to you. What is the cost of continuing to exhaust yourself just because you are uncomfortable asking for the much needed help you desire?

Tips for Effective Communication:

- Be transparent about your feelings and needs, even if you find them difficult to express. Let family members know if you are feeling tired, overwhelmed, or don't have enough support.

- Use "I" statements to convey your emotions and experiences without being judgmental. For example, "I really need two days to rest. Are you available next Thursday and Friday to sit with Dad from 12 p.m. – 8 p.m.?"

- Be specific with your request. I call it the "2DTP Model." When asking for help be specific with the date, duty, time, and place. For example: Are you available Thursday April 25th, to take mom to the dentist from 1 p.m. to 4 p.m. at Dr. XYZ's office?

- Actively listen to the perspectives and suggestions of others, even if they differ from your own. They provide insight to an ongoing challenge.

- Show gratitude for the support you received, no matter how small it may seem. Send a thank you text, email, or card. This gesture may be just the motivation needed for family members to provide ongoing support.

*Date:*_____

*Time:*_____

Chapter Reflections

1. One thought from this chapter that resonates with me is:

_____
_____
_____
_____
_____
_____

2. One concept from this chapter that I will implement within a week is:

_____
_____
_____
_____
_____
_____

3. One positive thought, affirmation, or kind word I want to say to myself today is:

_____
_____
_____
_____
_____
_____

Chapter 8: When Is Professional Assistance Needed?

Family and friends can provide support, however there may come a time when professional assistance is necessary to ensure the safety and well-being of your aging parent. Recognizing when it's time to seek professional help can be difficult but it is essential in providing the best possible care.

Remember your parents want to remain independent. They may not tell you they are missing payments on their bills, forgetting appointments, or no longer able to do household chores. Often parents won't tell you because they are afraid of being moved out of their home and placed in an assisted living facility. For this reason, you must be observant when visiting with your parents and note any indicators of the need for professional assistance.

Signs That Professional Assistance May Be Needed:

- The caregiver is having difficulty managing the parent's complex care requirements. For example, having to turn them over in the bed to change an adult diaper, having to physically carry them from one room to another, or getting them in and out of the shower or bathtub.

- You notice symptoms of your parents' physical or cognitive decline. This includes being unable to take care of personal hygiene needs like going to the restroom independently and forgetfulness of names, frequently losing their keys, and repeated conversations.

- Caregivers with ongoing feelings of being overwhelmed and fatigued despite hours of rest.

- Concerns about your parents' safety or quality of life at home. For instance, frequent falls, wandering from the home, not eating, and outbursts of anger and throwing objects.

Reach out to healthcare professionals, social workers, or home health care agencies for assistance if you're struggling to meet your parents' needs on your own. Asking for help is a sign of strength, not weakness.

Once you determine your family member needs professional care, include your parents in the interview and selection process. Having them participate in this process will prove to be paramount in establishing a positive caregiver and care receiver relationship.

"As you and your parents gently exchange roles, handle them with care. They are trying to manage uncertainty, sadness, and fear." Monica J. Gilliam

*Date:*_____

*Time:*_____

Chapter Reflections

1. One thought from this chapter that resonates with me is:

_____

_____

_____

_____

_____

2. One concept from this chapter that I will implement within a week is:

_____

_____

_____

_____

_____

3. One positive thought, affirmation, or kind word I want to say to myself today is:

_____

_____

_____

_____

_____

Chapter 9: Prioritizing Self-Care

As a care provider, it's easy to neglect your own needs while focusing on the well-being of your aging parent. Prioritizing self-care is not only essential for maintaining your own health but also for providing the best possible care for your loved one.

Prioritizing Self-Care: Why It's Important

Allow me to help someone today by saying self-care is not selfish; it's a necessary component of maintaining your physical, mental, and emotional health as a care provider. By prioritizing self-care, you'll be better equipped to handle the ups and downs of supporting your aging parent.

Incorporating self-care into your daily routine doesn't have to be complicated or time-consuming. Making time to engage in a hobby you enjoy such as reading or crossword puzzles or physical activities such as walking or going to the gym can help reduce stress, improve your mood, and boost your confidence as a caregiver.

Tips for Self-Care:

- **Meditation:** Take a few minutes each day to practice meditation, focusing on your breathing and redirecting negative thoughts. There are many free apps available to help you reach your place of Zen.

- **Exercise:** Incorporate regular physical activity into your weekly routine. Walking, jogging, yoga, and dancing are all great movement activities. Exercise benefits physical health, improves mood, and reduces stress. Contact your local community center to see if they offer free or discounted exercise classes.

- **Affirmations:** It is important to speak affirming, kind words to yourself daily. Remind yourself daily that you are strong, wise, patient, resilient, and beautiful. You have a beautiful soul to continue to care for an aging parent when they are most vulnerable.

- **Hobbies:** Make time for activities you enjoy like reading, gardening, painting, or golfing. Engaging in hobbies can provide a break from your caregiving tasks. Hobbies give you a sense of fulfillment and joy in the things you don't have time to do daily. It's like indulging in a hot fudge sundae on a summer day.

- **Nap Time:** I am all in for a good nap! Do not feel ashamed if sleeping is your self-care of choice. Oftentimes caregivers are sleep deprived because they always have something to do or are planning for the next task. If you want to sleep for a couple of hours, it is okay, friend.

- **Seeking Respite Care:** This wonderful service allows you to take time for yourself while ensuring your elderly parent receives the care and support they need. Giving yourself a well-deserved and much needed break by arranging for a neighbor or friend to take over your duties temporarily or exploring respite care services in your community is vital for preventing burnout and maintaining a positive attitude.

Date:_____

Time:_____

Chapter Reflections

1. One thought from this chapter that resonates with me is:

_____

_____

_____

_____

_____

_____

2. One concept from this chapter that I will implement within a week is:

_____

_____

_____

_____

_____

_____

3. One positive thought, affirmation, or kind word I want to say to myself today is:

_____

_____

_____

_____

_____

_____

Chapter 10: Overcoming Feelings of Guilt

Care providers may struggle with feelings of guilt when it comes to caring for loved ones. Some also struggle with the guilt of secretly not wanting to be the only or main support system for their parents. They often ask questions like "Why me?" or "Why are my siblings not carrying their share of the load?"

Most adult children taking care of their parents are in their 40s, 50s, or 60s. They had dreams of traveling, starting a business, retiring, or doing absolutely nothing. They looked forward to being an "empty nester." Now, all those dreams have been placed on hold indefinitely.

There could also be an internal conflict of "I want to pursue my dreams" versus "I need to do what is necessary for my parents." You are not alone in having those conflicting thoughts. Here is some good news for caregivers who feel burdened by guilt and mixed feelings. Below are a few ideas to help you renounce those feelings of guilt.

Tips for Overcoming Feelings of Guilt:

- Take time to process the "new normal" for your life. The more honest you are about your feelings in this situation, the more likely you are to adjust to the changes.

- Work to find the source of the guilt. Ask yourself if the guilt you are feeling is from a childhood issue, an adult issue, or is because you now lack autonomy. Once you identify the source you can start working toward addressing those feelings.

- Seek support from others who understand what you're going through and can offer empathy and encouragement.

- Give yourself permission to barely get by on some days and be okay with that decision. Accept that you are unable to do everything at an optimal level. Then work towards being comfortable with occasionally working at a functional level. Giving yourself this permission and practicing self-compassion will decrease your level of guilt.

"It's never too late to create a more positive family dynamic. Today is a good day to write a new family narrative."

Monica J. Gilliam

---

*Date:*_____

*Time:*_____

Chapter Reflections

1. One thought from this chapter that resonates with me is:

_____
_____
_____
_____
_____
_____

2. One concept from this chapter that I will implement within a week is:

_____
_____
_____
_____
_____
_____

3. One positive thought, affirmation, or kind word I want to say to myself today is:

_____
_____
_____
_____
_____
_____

Chapter 11: Navigating Healthcare and Community Resources

❋

As you become responsible for the care of your elderly parents, you may find navigating the healthcare system a little intimidating. To prepare for this venture, you'll want to know your parents' medical history and their maternal and paternal family medical history. Accessing medical information may be difficult in some communities because health issues were not openly discussed, or the medical records were poorly maintained. Gather as much medical information as possible. Talk with older family members and make note of any new health insights you discover.

For older parents with multiple healthcare needs, navigating the system can be difficult— especially when the use of technology is required for everything from viewing test results to communication with doctors. As their caregiver, managing their online health portal is another facet of healthcare you'll have to handle. As mentioned in chapter 6, now is the time to rely on the supportive healthcare professionals and community resources you've identified to help guide you. Understanding various healthcare options and resources available for seniors can help you make informed decisions that ensure your parent receives the care and support they need.

Tips for Healthcare Navigation and Resources:

- **Primary Care Physicians**: Establishing a relationship with your parent's primary care physician is good for managing their overall health and coordination of care. Before every doctor's appointment, make a list of the health concerns you have so you don't forget to ask these questions when you are in the exam room.

- **Specialists**: Depending on your parent's specific health needs, they may require care from specialists such as cardiologists, neurologists, or urologists. Having a primary care physician who specializes in the care of the elderly is a great option to explore.

- **Home Healthcare Services**: These services provide medical care and support in the comfort of your parent's home. Services may include speech therapy, physical therapy, and assistance with daily living activities. Please note if your parent is ambulatory and does not require skilled nursing care, you may have to pay "out-of-pocket" for these home health services.

- **Community Resources**: Many communities offer free support services for seniors, such as fitness programs, meal delivery, and medical transportation services. It is advised to research all senior services and programs before enrolling your loved ones.

- **Research Resources**: For a list of senior citizen program providers in your community, contact your local United Way Agency. Continue your due diligence by contacting the Better Business Bureau to determine if any formal complaints have been reported on the programs you are considering.

*Date:*_____

*Time:*_____

Chapter Reflections

1. One thought from this chapter that resonates with me is:

_____

_____

_____

_____

_____

_____

2. One concept from this chapter that I will implement within a week is:

_____

_____

_____

_____

_____

_____

3. One positive thought, affirmation, or kind word I want to say to myself today is:

_____

_____

_____

_____

_____

_____

Chapter 12: Managing Medical Appointments and Medications

Keeping track of appointments, adhering to prescribed medication dosage, and coordinating care between multiple healthcare providers requires excellent organization skills. There's nothing like getting your parents dressed for a doctor's appointment, finding a coveted handicap parking space, squeezing on the elevator with four other people, arriving to the office with a minute or two to spare and then getting to the front desk to find out you are there on the wrong day! This true story from my own experience is a case in point as to why organization is important when managing multiple appointments.

Anyone who has spent a Sunday afternoon filling your parents' pillbox is familiar with the routine of counting, recounting, then taking a pill out of one day and adding it to another day knows there's got to be a better way to manage this process. I have made charts, color coded charts, created spreadsheets, and checklists all in an effort to successfully do what I have dubbed as "pill patrol." Finding a system that works for you and your family really is a personal preference. The most important thing is to identify a system that works for you and stick to it.

Tips to Manage Medical Appointments and Medication:

- Keep a detailed record of your parents' medical history, including past surgeries with the dates, and medications with frequency and dosages. Make a list of all the medications and keep a photo of it on your phone.

- Review the expiration date on all medications. Discard expired medications. Most pharmacies have a program or service where you can safely dispose of expired or unused medications.

- Sign up for automatic medication refills.

- Request a three-month supply of prescriptions (ninety days). This will keep you from going to the pharmacy every thirty days for refills.

- Maintain a calendar to track upcoming medical appointments and procedures. Use whatever method works best for you whether it's the calendar app on your phone, a planner, or a wall calendar. I prefer to set a calendar reminder on my phone a week in advance. I also have a second reminder two days prior to the appointment.

- Create a medication management system to ensure your parents take their medications as prescribed, including organizing pills in pill boxes, setting up medication reminders on a phone, or printing a schedule and posting it in your parents' home.

- I highly recommend using a medication service that prepackages the pills individually with the date and time. All you will have to do is cut open the pill package for the appropriate day and time and give it to your loved one. You no longer have to spend time filling pill boxes. This service greatly reduces the possibility of errors when administering medication.

- Communicate with healthcare providers about your parent's needs and concerns. Ask questions or seek clarification about their care plan. Research their illnesses and use medical terms when possible. It has been my experience that the medical community is more engaged when I have knowledge of the diagnosis and possible treatment options.

- Make a list of the medications your parents are allergic to. Keep the list in a common area for easy access.

*Date:*_____

*Time:*_____

Chapter Reflections

1. One thought from this chapter that resonates with me is:

_____
_____
_____
_____
_____
_____

2. One concept from this chapter that I will implement within a week is:

_____
_____
_____
_____
_____
_____

3. One positive thought, affirmation, or kind word I want to say to myself today is:

_____
_____
_____
_____
_____
_____

Chapter 13: Being an Advocate for Your Parents

You are your parents' strongest advocate within the healthcare system. Advocating for your parents' needs involves speaking up, asking questions, and ensuring their voice is heard and respected by healthcare professionals. As the advocate for your parents, you will need to be their voice. Sometimes the pain they tell you they have can be dismissed as being related to old age, when in fact it could be an indication of something more serious.

It is important to be physically present for all your parents' medical appointments. Your presence serves many purposes. One of which is sending a clear message to the medical staff that your family is concerned and actively involved with the welfare of their elderly loved ones. Another reason for being in the room with your parents is because you provide an unspoken level of comfort for your parents. Additionally, you can act as an informal translator. During the appointment, you can take notes about what the doctor is saying, ask clarifying questions as needed, and then simplify complex explanations into a common language that your parents understand.

If you are unable to physically attend medical appointments with your parents, you can communicate with the physician via FaceTime or virtual platforms. Ask about telehealth services with your parents' insurance plan. Telehealth as a service, is another way to actively participate in your parents' healthcare. You can schedule appointments during your lunch hour or before going to work. This allows you to handle your caregiver duties and successfully manage your work responsibilities too.

Tips for Advocating for Your Parents:

- Educate yourself on your parent's health condition, treatment options, and patient rights.

- Prepare a list of questions and concerns to discuss with healthcare providers during appointments.

- Be assertive and persistent (not rude) in advocating for your parents' needs, by requesting additional tests, seeking a second opinion, or requesting a referral to a specialist.

- Keep detailed records of medical appointments, test results, and communication with healthcare providers to track your parent's progress and ensure continuity of care.

- Keep all medical records in one place. I suggest keeping the medication printout provided by the pharmacy. That information is a good reference regarding possible medication side effects.

Date:_____

Time:_____

Chapter Reflections

1. One thought from this chapter that resonates with me is:

_____

_____

_____

_____

_____

2. One concept from this chapter that I will implement within a week is:

_____

_____

_____

_____

_____

3. One positive thought, affirmation, or kind word I want to say to myself today is:

_____

_____

_____

_____

_____

Chapter 14: Planning for Their Future

Planning for your parents' future is a critical aspect of their well-being. Important considerations for planning ahead may include discussing end-of-life wishes, exploring options for long-term care, and coping with anticipatory grief. Having these conversations can be difficult, but they are necessary for ensuring your parent's preferences for medical care, and final requests are honored.

Additional discussions with your parents might include identifying a funeral home to handle their services. Will the body be buried or cremated? If cremated, who will have the ashes or does the parent want the ashes spread in a specific location? As the caregiver, it is imperative that you know the answers to all these questions before you have to implement them.

Tips for Discussing End-of-Life:

- Choose a time and place when you and your parents can have a private and uninterrupted conversation. You may want to go for a walk in the park, sit in the backyard, or talk around the kitchen table.

- Approach conversations with sensitivity, empathy, and an open mind. You can start by letting your parents know this is a difficult conversation for you. Tell them you recognize they are getting older and want to make sure you have a good understanding of what they want.

Let them know you want to start a conversation so you can all move forward as needed concerning their living arrangements, power of attorney designations, and final directives.

- Carefully listen to your parents' concerns, fears, and desires. Validate their feelings. Allow yourself to be vulnerable too. Let them know about your concerns and fears. Ways to comfort your parents during this conversation include holding their hands, putting your hands on their knees or rubbing their shoulders, and drying their tears. This is hard for your parents and will likely be hard for you too.

- Encourage your parents to document their directives in a living will and power of attorney document. Ask your parents if they are comfortable with you recording their wishes. If so, let them speak without coaxing from you or anyone else. Simply let them state what they want to happen.

- Seek an attorney or legal counsel of your choice to get legal advice regarding this topic and other legal matters such as wills, estate planning, power of attorney, etc.

*Date:*_____

*Time:*_____

Chapter Reflections

1. One thought from this chapter that resonates with me is:

_____

_____

_____

_____

_____

_____

2. One concept from this chapter that I will implement within a week is:

_____

_____

_____

_____

_____

_____

3. One positive thought, affirmation, or kind word I want to say to myself today is:

_____

_____

_____

_____

_____

_____

Chapter 15: Coping with Anticipatory Grief

$\ast$

Caring for an aging parent inevitably involves facing the reality of their eventual passing. This can evoke feelings of anticipatory grief and sadness. Coping with these emotions and preparing for the loss of a parent is an aspect of the caregiving journey that requires ongoing support. The support can come from a variety of sources including counseling, life coaching, and confidential talks with family, clergy, and other caregivers.

It is not uncommon for care providers to experience sleepless nights wondering when and how their loved one will transition. This thought is often in the back of the minds of every adult child taking care of their parents. The slightest cough, wobbly step, or shaky hand leads you to wonder if their life is nearing an end.

One thing that will help manage grief is having a plan. As discussed in the last chapter, you need to know your parent's preferences, wants, and needs. What course of action will you take if hospitalization or hospice is required? Who do you need to call? What funeral home will handle arrangements? Having an answer to these uncomfortable but important questions will give you the time and space to focus on grieving the loss of a loved one instead of worrying and being stressed about not being prepared or knowing what decisions need to be made.

There is no easy way to prepare for the loss of a parent. Educate yourself on the five stages (seven stages for chronic disease) of grief. Become familiar with the stages so you will be better able to identify the emotions you are feeling. Interestingly, the five stages of grief may not happen in order, nor will every person experience all the stages. Grieving is as complex and personal as the individual who is experiencing it.

Tips for Coping with Anticipatory Grief:

- Allow yourself to experience a range of emotions including depression, anger, or fear.

- Educate yourself on your loved one's illness. Don't live in denial about the health status of your parents.

- Know if there is a life expectancy associated with the diagnosed illness.

- Engage in meaningful activities and traditions that honor your parent's life and legacy.

- Establish a scholarship in honor of your parents.

- Create a non-profit organization that addresses your parents' social concerns.

- Chronicle family activities with videos and photos. It's not too late to make good family memories.

- Ask for and give forgiveness for any lingering feelings of hurt or anger.

Date:_____

Time:_____

Chapter Reflections

1. One thought from this chapter that resonates with me is:

_____

_____

_____

_____

_____

_____

2. One concept from this chapter that I will implement within a week is:

_____

_____

_____

_____

_____

_____

3. One positive thought, affirmation, or kind word I want to say to myself today is:

_____

_____

_____

_____

_____

_____

Words of Encouragement for All Caregivers

Caring for an aging parent can be one of the most challenging yet rewarding experiences of your life. What an honor it is to take care of the ones who took care of you. They wiped your tears, took you to practice, paid tuition, cooked your favorite meal, and taught you how to ride a bike. I know not all parent and child relationships have a positive history, but now is a wonderful opportunity to heal any past hurts and move forward. There is no time for blaming or finger pointing, just compassion for elderly parents who did the best they could with the knowledge and emotional capacity they had at that time. Give yourself and your parents the phenomenal gift of grace. We all need it. And with it you can successfully navigate this amazing role of caregiver with compassion and dignity.

Thank you for your dedication and love in caring for your parents.

www.ingramcontent.com/pod-product-compliance
Lightning Source LLC
LaVergne TN
LVHW051818080426
835513LV00017B/1998

* 9 7 9 8 8 9 4 0 1 0 3 3 5 *